BLIZZARDS

MICHAEL WOODS AND MARY B. WOODS

LERNER PUBLICATIONS COMPANY
MINNEAPOLIS

To Margaret Woods

Editor's note: Determining the exact death toll following disasters is often difficult—if not impossible—especially in the case of disasters that took place long ago. The authors and the editors in this series have used their best judgment in determining which figures to include.

Lerner Publications Company
A division of Lerner Publishing Group, Inc.
241 First Avenue North
Minneapolis, MN 55401 USA

For reading leveles and more information,
look up this title at www.lernerbooks.com.

Library of Congress Cataloging-in-Publication Data

Woods, Michael, 1946–
        Blizzards / by Michael Woods and Mary B. Woods.
            p. cm. — (Disasters up close)
        Includes bibliographical references and index.
        ISBN 978–0–8225–6575–8 (lib. bdg. : alk. paper)
        ISBN 978–0–7613–3974–8 (eBook)
        1. Blizzards—Juvenile literature. I. Woods, Mary B. (Mary Boyle), 1946–
    II. Title.
        QC926.37.W66 2008
        551.55'5–dc22   2006031496

Manufactured in the United States of America
2 – VI – 11/1/13

Contents

Introduction

IN FEBRUARY 2003, A SEVERE WINTER STORM FORMED IN THE CENTRAL UNITED STATES. IT HEADED EAST, DUMPING SNOW ON ILLINOIS, OHIO, AND MANY OTHER STATES. MEANWHILE, ANOTHER STRONG STORM WAS HOWLING UP THE EAST COAST. HEAVY RAIN AND HIGH WINDS BLEW THROUGH NORTH CAROLINA AND SOUTH CAROLINA. ON FEBRUARY 16, THE TWO STORMS JOINED. THEY FORMED A BLIZZARD THAT SWEPT THROUGH THE NORTHEAST THE NEXT DAY—PRESIDENTS' DAY. THIS MONSTER SNOWSTORM BROUGHT LIFE TO A STANDSTILL FOR MILLIONS OF PEOPLE.

Nearly 2 feet (0.6 meters) of snow fell on Washington, D.C.; Boston; and other cities. The snow would have been bad enough by itself. But the storm also brought winds up to 50 miles (80 kilometers) per hour. Wind whipped the thick snow through the air. People could barely see through it.

"It's no man's land out there," said Paul McIntyre, who lived in Maryland. "It looks more like Siberia [a famously snowy part of Russia] than Maryland."

Cars rear-ended one another because drivers could not see. Trucks flipped over and skidded off roads into ditches. "It's been horrendous," said Joey Caserta, whose tow truck helped rescue drivers in New York City. "It's like oil on the [road] with all that snow on top of the icy asphalt."

Travelers make their way through whiteout conditions along the coast in Boston on February 17, 2003.

4

The blizzard forced airlines to cancel thousands of flights. Travelers trapped in airport terminals had to sleep on the floor. Lynn Anderson's vacation was ruined when the blizzard stranded her in Philadelphia. "It's turned into a complete nightmare," she said. Many travelers felt similarly.

With snow blocking sidewalks, driveways, and roads, millions of people were stuck in their homes. The fierce winds knocked down power and phone lines. More than 250,000 homes and stores in a dozen states lost electricity. That meant no lights, no TV, and no Internet. Some people ran out of food. They were snowed in and could not go grocery shopping.

Snow blocked some streets in Washington, D.C., for three days. "Once you've plowed this stuff, where do you dump these mountains of [snow]?" asked District of Columbia mayor Anthony Williams. Cities spent almost $100 million to clear roads and repair damage from the storm.

For some, the storm caused the worst kind of loss—it killed at least twenty-eight people. Most died in car accidents. Some got lost outdoors in the blinding snow and froze to death. Others died from heart attacks while shoveling snow. The blizzard was the most crippling snowstorm to hit the Northeast in years.

People in Georgetown, Maryland, drive cautiously during a 2003 blizzard.

"It's turned into a complete nightmare."

—Lynn Anderson, who was stranded in Philadelphia by the February 2003 blizzard

What Are Blizzards?

BLIZZARDS ARE WINTER STORMS WITH HEAVY SNOW, STRONG WINDS, AND BONE-CHILLING COLD. THAT THREE-IN-ONE WEATHER COMBINATION MAKES BLIZZARDS THE MOST DANGEROUS KIND OF WINTER STORMS.

With snow swirling through the air, visibility (the distance people can see) is very low. People driving cars or walking cannot see the road well. Temperatures in these storms often drop below 0°F (−18°C). And high winds make the cold feel colder. A person's skin can freeze in seconds.

To be called a blizzard, a storm must have low temperatures, winds of at least 35 miles (56 km) per hour, and a lot of falling or blowing snow. The snow must reduce visibility to less than 0.25 miles (0.4 km) for three hours or more.

Severe blizzards are rare and extremely dangerous. In a severe blizzard, winds blow at 45 miles (72 km) per hour or more. Dense snow falls or drifts in the wind. Temperatures fall to 10°F (−12°C) or less.

SNOW DAYS

Every year blizzards shut down cities and towns in many areas of the world. Roads and airports may close. Children get a snow day if roads are too dangerous for school buses. A 2003 blizzard in Colorado and Wyoming snowed in more than 3.5 million people.

SNOW SHUTTLE

In the 1980s, the former Soviet Union (modern Russia and many neighboring countries) built a spaceship similar to a U.S. space shuttle. They called the spaceship Buran—the same name as the fast winds that howl in Russian snowstorms.

These Montana residents didn't let a 2003
blizzard keep them at home. They used
snowmobiles and skis to get around.

People may be stuck in their homes for days. A blizzard can make those days uncomfortable. People often run short of food. Wind may knock down power, telephone, and cable lines. That means no lights, food spoiling in the fridge, and maybe no heat in the house. Television? E-mail? Forget it.

DANGEROUS STORMS

Blizzards kill or injure hundreds of people every year. Car accidents cause many of the deaths and injuries. Some people freeze to death in cars stuck in snowdrifts. Others die after getting lost outdoors in blinding snow. People, especially the sick and elderly, may even freeze to death at home if the heat goes off. Blizzards also injure and kill farm animals and pets left outside.

Fires are another danger in blizzards, despite the snow all around. Fire can spread easily in the wind, and water in fire hoses may freeze before a fire is put out. In addition, fire trucks, ambulances, and police cars often cannot get through the snow to reach people in emergencies.

Blizzards can be expensive. Plowing streets costs cities millions of dollars each year. Heavy snow can make roofs fall in. Damaged power lines need repair. And when stores and businesses close, the owners and workers lose money.

MORE BLIZZARDS AHEAD?

Blizzards have caused trouble for humans for thousands of years. Some scientists think that we may have more frequent and worse blizzards in the future. Earth's temperature has been slowly rising for many years, bringing warmer winters. Scientists think air pollution may be causing or speeding up this phenomenon, called global warming. Warmer air can hold more moisture. Air eventually releases its moisture as rain or snow. So warmer winters mean more chances for blizzards to form.

BIG SNOW IN THE BIG CITY

New York City spends $1 million on snow removal for every inch of snow that covers its streets. Removing snow that fell in a 2003 blizzard cost almost $20 million.

A plow removes snow from a Manhattan, New York, street after a snowstorm dropped more than 2 feet (0.6 m) of snow on the city.

"**As mighty a snow** as perhaps has been known in the **memory of man,** is at this time **lying on the ground.**"

—Minister and author Cotton Mather, writing about a 1717 New England blizzard with snowdrifts 25 feet (7.6 m) high

Fierce winds made snow fall sideways in New York during the 1888 blizzard.

March 11–13, 1888
THE GREAT BLIZZARD OF 1888

Warm rain was falling in New York City on Sunday, March 11, 1888, as Meta Lilienthal said goodnight to her parents. *"When I opened my eyes early next morning . . . I became dimly aware of something unusual,"* Lilienthal remembered. *"I rushed into my parents' bedroom and shouted, 'Father, mother, we are having a blizzard!'"*

The same storm surprised millions of others from Maryland to Maine. People could see just a short distance ahead through winds of 70 miles (113 km) per hour. Only about 2 feet (0.6 m) of snow fell on New York City, but the drifts piled up to 20 feet (6 m) high.

A. C. Chadbourne's train from Boston got stuck in a drift as it reached New York. So he started walking. *"I . . . remember being blown down twice while crossing Broadway and crawling through the snow on my hands and knees up to the . . . sidewalk,"* Chadbourne said.

Other passengers couldn't get out of elevated trains that were stuck on tracks high above the street. Rescuers put ladders up to the tracks so people could escape. Climbing down was difficult in the blowing snow. Some passengers slipped and fell.

The snow trapped some workers inside their building on Long Island. Shamgar Babcock remembered how they finally got out. *"We . . . did have two shovels,"* he said. *"It was necessary to tunnel through for about 15 feet [4.6 m], carrying the snow upstairs and throwing it out of the back windows."*

On Monday night, New York was dark. The storm had knocked down electric wires. Pipes that carried natural gas, which people burned in lamps to light their homes, froze and burst. By Tuesday morning, the temperature was −5°F (−21°C). Many people ran out of coal to burn for heat. They were freezing indoors.

As the blizzard continued, food ran out. In those days, there were no refrigerators. Trucks delivered milk to homes, and people shopped for food every day. But in the blizzard, milk trucks couldn't get through and people could not get to stores.

Fire trucks couldn't get through the snow either. Fires caused about $25 million in damage—almost $500 million in modern money.

About three hundred people died in the blizzard. At least one hundred more died at sea, when huge waves and winds of 90 miles (145 km) per hour overturned their boats. The storm damaged or sunk about two hundred ships on the Atlantic Ocean.

"**Jumping from my bed,** I went to the window . . . and then I stood **motionless, speechless.**"

—Meta Lilienthal, on the Great Blizzard of 1888

Snowdrifts from the blizzard stalled trains. Many train passengers were forced to walk to the next station.

What Causes Blizzards?

SUNNY SKIES TURN STORMY BECAUSE BIG MASSES (AREAS) OF AIR MOVE ACROSS THE LAND. THESE AIR MASSES ARE CALLED WEATHER SYSTEMS. THEY MAY STRETCH FOR HUNDREDS OF MILES.

Each weather system contains its own set of weather conditions. One system may be rainy. Another might bring dry conditions. Blizzards usually form when a warm, moist weather system and a cold, dry system bump into each other.

TROUBLEMAKER

Cold, dry weather systems provide the freezing temperatures that accompany blizzards. Warm, moist systems provide moisture for snow to form. Warm air is lighter than cold air. So when warm air and cold air meet, the warm air rises above the cold air.

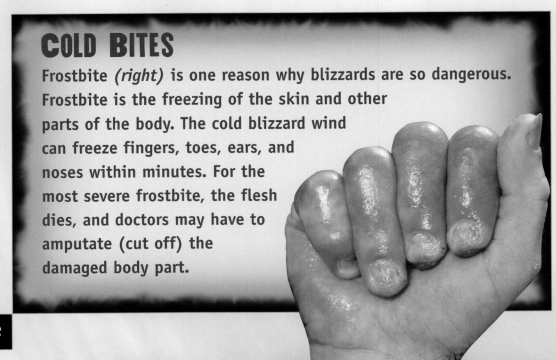

COLD BITES

Frostbite *(right)* is one reason why blizzards are so dangerous. Frostbite is the freezing of the skin and other parts of the body. The cold blizzard wind can freeze fingers, toes, ears, and noses within minutes. For the most severe frostbite, the flesh dies, and doctors may have to amputate (cut off) the damaged body part.

BLIZZARD WEATHER

snowflakes form
and fall through
cold air

moving air creates
strong winds

warm air flows up
and over cold air

cold air flows
under warm air

As the warm air rises, it cools and forms clouds of moisture. The air becomes so cool that moisture in the clouds turns into snow. The snow falls to the ground. It falls mostly through the cold air swooping under the warm air. So the snow never melts into rain.

At the same time, air along the ground rushes in to replace the rising warm air. Then more air rushes in to replace the air along the ground. The rushing air is the wind that blows snow in a blizzard.

The worst blizzards form when very different air masses meet. A very cold, dry air mass running into a very warm, wet air mass can make a terrible blizzard. The storm will have plenty of moving air to form strong winds and plenty of moisture for heavy snow.

JET STREAMS

Special winds help steer weather systems. These winds are called jet streams. Jet streams are strong wind currents that blow about 20,000 feet (6,096 m) above Earth's surface. They can howl at more than 100 miles (161 km) per hour.

Jet streams push air masses onto the collision course that forms blizzards. Once a blizzard forms, jet streams also help steer the storm from one place to another.

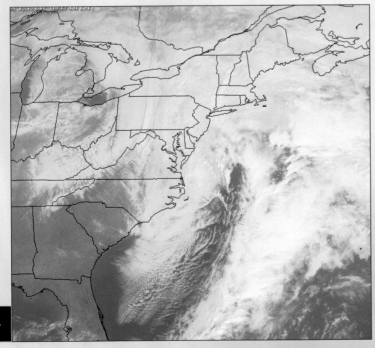

An enhanced satellite image shows a large winter storm over the eastern United States in 2001.

A jet stream, such as this one over Egypt and the Red Sea, can move clouds at more than 100 miles (161 km) per hour.

ALBERTA CLIPPERS AND NASTY NOR'EASTERS

Alberta Clippers are cold storms, often with strong winds of 40 miles (64 km) per hour. These storms form in the Canadian province of Alberta and travel southeast into North Dakota, South Dakota, and Minnesota. Then they usually head eastward toward the Great Lakes. Before reaching the lakes, Clippers don't pick up very much moisture. So they usually cause little snowfall.

Once in a while, however, Alberta Clippers help create terrible blizzards. This happens when a Clipper moves east to the Atlantic Ocean. As it sails over the Atlantic, the Clipper may meet another storm moving north from the Gulf of Mexico. If the two storms join, they form a blizzard called a nor'easter.

In the winter, nor'easters bring frigid air and strong winds from Canada. The combination of those winds with moisture from the Gulf of Mexico has caused some of the worst blizzards in history, such as the 1993 Superstorm. In that storm, a nor'easter dumped 3 to 4 feet (0.9 to 1.2 m) of snow on parts of the East Coast.

VERY FUNNY!

After the Great Blizzard of 1888, people put up funny signs in New York and other cities. One sign read, "Do You Get My Drift?" Signs stuck in the middle of deep snowdrifts said, "Keep Off the Grass" or "Don't Pick the Flowers."

MINIBLIZZARDS

Winds that blow over big lakes pick up moisture. If the wind is cold, the moisture it picks up becomes snow. Once the wind reaches shore, it can cause a miniblizzard, called a lake-effect snowstorm. These storms dump heavy snow on a small area of land. One town may get 4 feet (1.2 m) of snow, while people living several miles away get none.

The falling snow may be thick enough to cause a whiteout. In a whiteout, everything looks white because the air is filled with snow. Visibility is almost zero. People who go outside may get lost and freeze to death. Driving in a whiteout is dangerous. Sometimes chain-reaction accidents occur, in which multiple cars smash into one another.

"Some of the drifts were very high, but I had no means of knowing just how many feet. I do know, however, that **I walked clean over the tops** of what I knew to be **fairly tall trees."**

—Herbert Smith, who lived in New York City during the Great Blizzard of 1888

The 1888 blizzard was the largest to hit the eastern United States in the nineteenth century. It brought New York City to a standstill.

After the Armistice Day Blizzard in 1940, people helped shovel massive amounts of snow from roads.

November 11, 1940
MIDWESTERN UNITED STATES

People in Minnesota were used to seeing ducks flying overhead every autumn. Ducks migrate over that state while heading south from Canada for the winter. But on November 11, 1940, people couldn't believe how many ducks were in the air.

"I never saw anything like it," said Ray Sherin, who was fourteen years old that fall. *"Ducks were flying so low . . . I knew something was coming."*

The ducks knew what was about to happen. They were trying to escape one of the most terrible blizzards of the twentieth century.

The storm totally surprised people throughout the Midwest, however. November 11 began with temperatures above 60°F (16°C) in parts of Minnesota. But by afternoon, temperatures had plunged below freezing. Snow fell, and winds howling at 60 miles (97 km) per hour piled the snow into drifts 8 feet (2.4 m) deep. One newspaper called the storm "the winds of hell."

Della Osendorf, thirteen, and her father struggled through the snow toward their barn. When Della arrived, her father was no longer behind her.

> "When I got there, **I saw the awful truth.**
> My god! Two of those **iron horses** [trains] ...
> **smashed** right head on together."
>
> —Wendelin Beckers, on finding two trains that
> collided during the 1940 Armistice Day Blizzard

Afraid that he was lost in the storm, Della went looking for him. She disappeared. The next day, neighbors found Della frozen to death in a snowdrift. Her father? He had been lost for only a few minutes before finding his way into the barn.

James Bice was playing cards at home in Watkins, Minnesota, during the storm. *"All at once, we heard a bang like a thunderbolt . . . and the ground just trembled,"* he remembered. Two trains, roaring through the snow, had crashed head-on into each other. Because of whiteout conditions, the crew of one train hadn't seen the signal to switch tracks. Two passengers died. *"One of the whistles . . . got jammed and it let out the most mournful tone,"* said Wendelin Beckers, who had been at work nearby. The whistle kept blowing all day. People said it sounded like the train was crying for the blizzard's victims.

The storm raged for two days. It was nicknamed the Armistice Day Blizzard because of the national holiday on which it began. That holiday is called Veterans' Day in modern times. More than 150 people died, including 49 in Minnesota. Many were duck hunters who froze. *"Nobody had heavy clothes,"* said Brian Cafferty, a resident of central Minnesota. *"It was so warm that morning. . . . [Then] the snow just kept getting heavier, heavier, and heavier, and blowing, blowing, and blowing, until you didn't see anything."*

This train derailed during the 1940 blizzard.

Blizzard Country

BLIZZARDS CAN FORM WHEREVER WINTERS GET VERY COLD AND SNOWY—IN AREAS FAR FROM THE EQUATOR OR HIGH UP IN MOUNTAINS. BLIZZARDS FREQUENTLY STRIKE ALASKA, NORTHERN CANADA, ANTARCTICA, AND SIBERIA. BUT MOST PARTS OF THESE AREAS ARE SO COLD THAT FEW PEOPLE LIVE THERE, SO STORMS THERE USUALLY DO NOT CAUSE DISASTERS. IN A DISASTER, MANY PEOPLE MAY BE KILLED OR INJURED. HOMES, STORES, AND OTHER BUILDINGS MAY BE DESTROYED. THE DAMAGE FROM A DISASTER MAY COST BILLIONS OF DOLLARS.

In the United States, winter storms can drop snow on many parts of the country. But most blizzards hit only in certain areas. One of these places is the northern Great Plains, a huge, flat area east of the Rocky Mountains. The northern Great Plains covers parts of Colorado, Kansas, Nebraska, Wyoming, Montana, South Dakota, and North Dakota. The Canadian provinces of Saskatchewan, Alberta, and part of Manitoba also lie in the Great Plains.

FAST FACT

South Dakota gets so many blizzards that it sometimes is called the Blizzard State.

BLIZZARD CITIES

Another blizzard zone includes a broad area of the midwestern and northeastern United States. It stretches from Minnesota through the Great Lakes and east to New York, Massachusetts, and Maine. Blizzards in this area often become disasters because they affect so many cities, including Chicago, Boston, and New York.

People living to the east or south of the Great Lakes are in the zone of heavy lake-effect snowstorms. The worst of these storms occur in cities such as Erie, Pennsylvania; Muskegon, Michigan; South Bend, Indiana; and Buffalo,

Syracuse, and Rochester in New York. Areas near the Great Salt Lake in Utah also experience lake-effect storms.

BLIZZARDS AROUND THE WORLD

Blizzards cause disasters in many other areas of the world too. In Europe, blizzards are common in the Alps. This great mountain range stretches through Austria, Switzerland, France, Italy, and other countries. Blizzards also occur in Great Britain, Greece, and Scandinavian countries such as Norway and Sweden.

DID YOU KNOW?

Syracuse Hancock Airport in Syracuse, New York, owns the world's biggest snowplow. The plow's blade, the part that clears the path, is 4 feet (1.2 m) high and 32 feet (9.8 m) wide. That's almost as long as a school bus.

People in the Himalaya Mountains, in Asia, experience terrible blizzards. These people live in the countries of Bhutan, China, India, Nepal, and Pakistan. Russia is famous for its harsh winters and blizzards as well.

Blizzards also can happen in Turkey, Afghanistan, and Iraq. In 1972 one of the worst blizzards in history killed four thousand people in Iran.

Residents of Shandong Province, China, fight against a blizzard in December 2005.

DISASTER ZONES

Blizzards occur in many cold parts of the world. But blizzards cause disasters only when they affect large numbers of people. This map shows where some of the worst blizzard disasters have occurred. The boxed information describes disasters discussed in this book.

EUROPE—1956
EUROPE—2005

EUROPE

ASIA

INNER MONGOLIA, CHINA, 2000–2001 (at least 39 deaths)

SINKIANG PROVINCE, CHINA—1999

AFRICA

AUSTRALIA

NORTH AMERICA

EASTERN UNITED STATES, 1993 (about 270 deaths)

MIDWEST UNITED STATES, 1940 (150 deaths)

TRUCKEE PASS, CALIFORNIA, UNITED STATES; 1846–1847 (about 100 deaths)

NORTHEAST UNITED STATES; 1888 (at least 400 deaths), 2003 (at least 28 deaths)

MIDWEST UNITED STATES, 1888 (about 500 deaths)

CHICAGO—1967

NORTHEAST UNITED STATES—1996

WASHINGTON, D.C., UNITED STATES; 1922 (at least 98 deaths)

SOUTH AMERICA

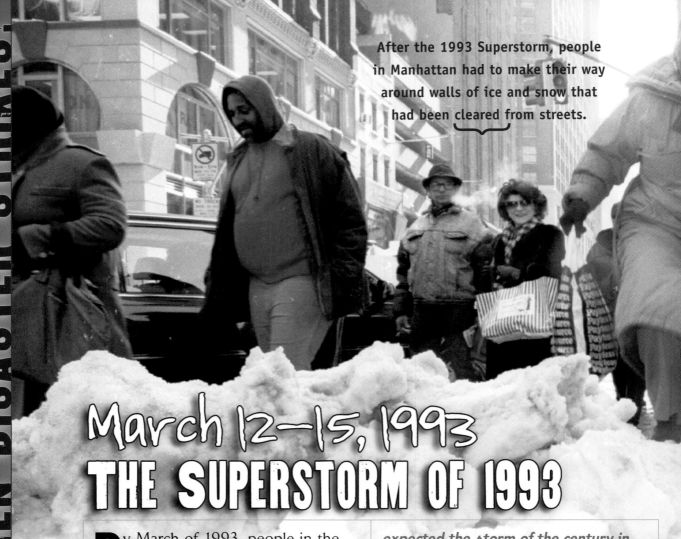

After the 1993 Superstorm, people in Manhattan had to make their way around walls of ice and snow that had been cleared from streets.

March 12–15, 1993
THE SUPERSTORM OF 1993

By March of 1993, people in the eastern United States were looking forward to spring. It had been a long, cold winter. But it was not over yet. Freezing air was pouring into the area from Canada. On March 12, that cold air mass met a warm, wet weather system from the Gulf of Mexico. The air masses joined and formed the worst U.S. blizzard since 1888. The storm affected 130 million people in twenty-six states, from Florida to Maine.

Some parts of Tennessee got 4.7 feet (1.4 m) of snow. *"Whoever expected the storm of the century in March?"* said Marseata Lockhart, who lived in Tennessee. *"We thought, 'Oh, right, a little snow.' Then 24 inches [61 cm] fell."* In other parts of the South, where winter usually is warm, people struggled through waist-deep snow.

Winds as strong as 100 miles (161 km) per hour knocked down trees, branches, and power lines. When the wires came down, the electricity went out—for more than 3 million people.

The storm stranded some people in homes on mountaintops and other hard-to-reach areas. Police feared those

The Superstorm hit as far south as Georgia *(right)* and Florida.

people would freeze to death. But not even rugged military Humvees could drive through the snow to rescue them. *"We're sending [rescue workers] on horses to get in to the remote places,"* explained Rudy Roach, a sheriff in Georgia.

Snow also piled up on roofs. Sometimes the snow was so heavy that a roof collapsed. That was the case at one school in New York City. *"The damage is [tremendous],"* remarked Rabbi Yerachmiel Barash, who worked at the school.

Many airports and roads were closed. Blowing snow made it impossible for drivers to see, stranding travelers on roads and in motels and airports.

When the storm ended, people still were stranded. Although the roads had been plowed, snow trapped cars in driveways and buried them on streets. Maurice Thomas, co-owner of a snowplowing service in Freeport, New York, remembered people in tears calling him for help. *"I have people crying that they can't get to work tomorrow,"* he said.

Even worse, about 270 people died in the Superstorm. Hundreds more were injured. Altogether, the blizzard caused $3 billion to $6 billion in damage.

"Whoever expected the storm of the century in March?"

—*Marseata Lockhart, who lived in Tennessee during the 1993 Superstorm*

Measuring the Menace

WHEN A BLIZZARD IS APPROACHING, PEOPLE ASK QUESTIONS. HOW BAD WILL THE STORM BE? HOW LONG WILL IT LAST? ANSWERING THOSE QUESTIONS CAN HELP PEOPLE PREPARE FOR A BLIZZARD. THEY BUY EXTRA FOOD, FLASHLIGHTS, AND BATTERIES. ROAD WORKERS CAN CALL OUT MORE SNOWPLOWS TO CLEAR THE ROADS. THE ELECTRIC COMPANY CAN ALERT WORKERS TO FIX POWER LINES KNOCKED DOWN DURING THE STORM.

Meteorologists (people who study and predict the weather) have several ways of knowing when a blizzard is approaching. Doppler radar uses radio waves to monitor moisture in clouds and snow or rain over a large area. This radar can measure how much snow is falling inside a storm. It also measures wind speed. So it can detect which storms may have wind and snow fierce enough to be a blizzard.

This weather satellite collects data and sends it to meteorologists so they can better predict the weather.

Satellites that orbit Earth also help forecasters predict the weather. The satellites measure temperature, wind, and moisture all over Earth. Then computer models (programs) use that information to predict weather over several days. The models show where a blizzard is likely to hit.

Meteorologists rely partly on weather services such as the U.S. National Weather Service. These organizations use the most advanced computer models to create large-scale predictions. Reports from weather stations in other areas help forecasters too. Forecasters track the direction of a storm. Then they can warn people who live in its path.

A meteorologist uses computer models to predict weather patterns.

SIZING UP SNOW

Meteorologists take measurements during and after a storm to find out how big it was. Measuring a blizzard means checking temperatures, wind speeds, and snow depth. Measuring snow depth in a blizzard can be difficult because of snowdrifts. The drifts often are much higher than the actual snowfall level.

Meteorologists use special instruments to measure how much snow falls and how fast it is falling. A tool called a Hotplate snow gauge measures snowfall by monitoring two metal plates that are stacked on top of each other. The wind cools both plates. Falling snow also cools the top plate. But the plates are heated to stay at a constant temperature. So when it snows, the top plate takes more energy to keep it at the same temperature than the bottom plate does. Scientists compare the energy needed for each plate to maintain the same temperature.

SNOWY CITIES

Buffalo, New York, holds the record among big cities for the most snow in a single winter. During the winter of 1976–1977, Buffalo got 16.6 feet (5.1 m) of snow. Rochester, New York, comes in second, with 13.4 feet (4.1 m) in one winter, and Portland, Maine, third with 11.8 feet (3.6 m).

SNOWIEST U.S. MOUNTAINS

A record 95 feet (29 m) of snow fell on the Mount Baker Ski Area in northwestern Washington State during the 1998–1999 snowfall season. The previous U.S. record was 93.5 feet (28.5 m). It was set during the winter of 1971–1972 at Mount Rainier, about 150 miles (241 km) south of Mount Baker.

Mount Baker is part of the Cascade Mountain range in the Pacific Northwest.

Skiers enjoy the snow at Mount Baker Ski Area in Washington State.

From that measurement, they can tell exactly how much snow has fallen each minute.

Simpler instruments also provide accurate measurements. An instrument called a snowboard is merely a flat piece of wood. It is placed on the ground in the open, away from buildings, fences, and other places where drifts pile up. A person takes a measurement by pushing a ruler or yardstick down through the snow to the board. Weather observers are volunteers who help the National Weather Service measure snowfall in different areas. They often use snowboards for their measurements.

The anemometer is the main instrument scientists use to measure wind speed. A simple anemometer catches the wind in three cups. The wind spins the cups. The stronger the wind is, the faster the cups spin.

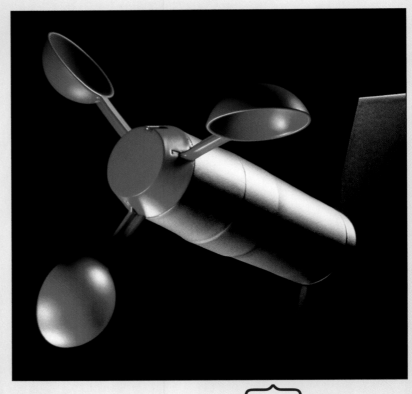

An anemometer

Thermometers measure temperature. Meteorologists use two kinds of thermometers to get very accurate readings: one for high temperatures and one for low.

WINDCHILL TEMPERATURE INDEX

When wind blows on the skin, it draws heat from the body. That's why the breeze from a fan feels good in hot weather. But wind also makes low temperatures feel even colder. Wind blowing at 15 miles (24 km) per hour makes an air temperature of 0°F (−18°C) feel like −19°F (−28°C). The wind's effect on temperature is called the windchill factor.

Exposed skin is especially at risk for frostbite during the high winds of blizzards, such as in this New York blizzard in 2006.

WINDCHILL

This chart shows how cold the air feels when the wind blows at different speeds.

							Temperature (°F)											
Calm	40	35	30	25	20	15	10	5	0	-5	-10	-15	-20	-25	-30	-35	-40	-45
5	36	31	25	19	13	7	1	-5	-11	-16	-22	-28	-34	-40	-46	-52	-57	-63
10	34	27	21	15	9	3	-4	-10	-16	-22	-28	-35	-41	-47	-53	-59	-66	-72
15	32	25	19	13	6	0	-7	-13	-19	-26	-32	-39	-45	-51	-58	-64	-71	-77
20	30	24	17	11	4	-2	-9	-15	-22	-29	-35	-42	-48	-55	-61	-68	-74	-81
25	29	23	16	9	3	-4	-11	-17	-24	-31	-37	-44	-51	-58	-64	-71	-78	-84
30	28	22	15	8	1	-5	-12	-19	-26	-33	-39	-46	-53	-60	-67	-73	-80	-87
35	28	21	14	7	0	-7	-14	-21	-27	-34	-41	-48	-55	-62	-69	-76	-82	-89
40	27	20	13	6	-1	-8	-15	-22	-29	-36	-43	-50	-57	-64	-71	-78	-84	-91
45	26	19	12	5	-2	-9	-16	-23	-30	-37	-44	-51	-58	-65	-72	-79	-86	-93
50	26	19	12	4	-3	-10	-17	-24	-31	-38	-45	-52	-60	-67	-74	-81	-88	-95
55	25	18	11	4	-3	-11	-18	-25	-32	-39	-46	-54	-61	-68	-75	-82	-89	-97
60	25	17	10	3	-4	-11	-19	-26	-33	-40	-48	-55	-62	-69	-76	-84	-91	-98

Wind (mph)

Frostbite Times   ■ 30 minutes   ■ 10 minutes   ■ 5 minutes

$$\text{Wind Chill (°F)} = 35.74 + 0.6215T - 35.75(V^{0.16}) + 0.4275T(V^{0.16})$$

Where, T= Air Temperature (°F) V= Wind Speed (mph)

Effective 11/01/01

High winds can turn cold weather into dangerous conditions. Windchill reports from weather centers give people important warnings about the risk of frostbite in a blizzard. When the windchill is very low, skin can freeze in minutes.

NESIS SCALE

In 2004 scientists at the National Weather Service and the Weather Channel, a weather news TV network, developed a scale to rank snowstorms. On the Northeast Snowfall Impact Scale (NESIS), a storm is classified into one of five categories after it ends. The storm's rank is based on the amount of snowfall, the size of the area it affected, and the number of people that live in the storm's path. Classifying a storm lets meteorologists compare it to other storms.

The scale only ranks storms that hit the Northeast. That's because most people who are affected by severe snowstorms in the United States live in that area. And when storms delay flights in and out of the Northeast, it impacts people and businesses throughout the country.

SNOW SHOVEL JOHN

On March 9, 1888, John J. Meisinger bought three thousand snow shovels to sell in his store in New York City. The newspaper ran a story making fun of him. New York had experienced its warmest winter in years. Spring was on the way. People didn't think anybody would buy those shovels. They jokingly called him Snow Shovel John. Two days later, the worst blizzard in history hit New York. Meisinger sold every one of the shovels.

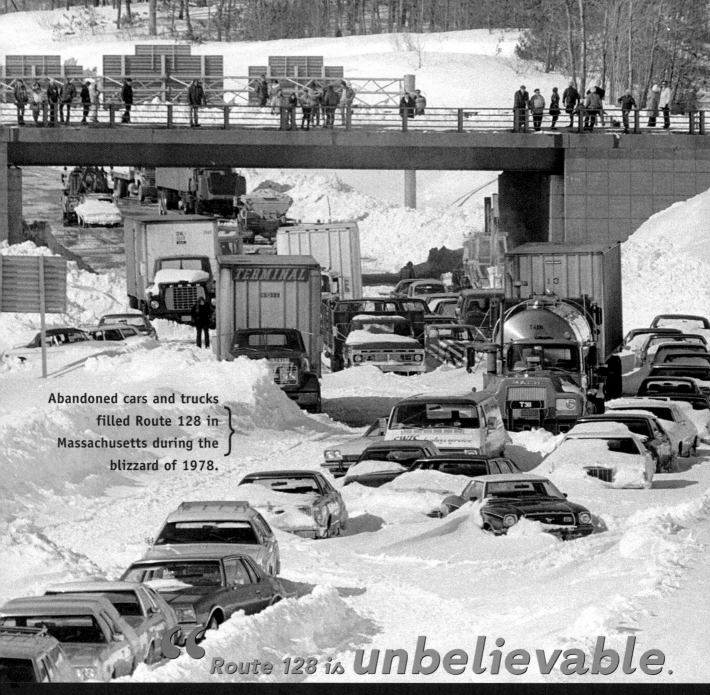

Abandoned cars and trucks filled Route 128 in Massachusetts during the blizzard of 1978.

"Route 128 is **unbelievable**. It is as if there has been a massive rush-hour traffic jam and somebody said, '*Stop*' and covered the cars with *5 feet [1.5 m] of snow*."

—Massachusetts governor Michael Dukakis, speaking about the snowfall after a 1978 blizzard

After blizzards struck Inner Mongolia in early 2001, trucks brought in emergency food for livestock.

December 31, 2000
CHINA

People living in Inner Mongolia, in northern China, are used to severe winters. But starting on December 31, 2000, they experienced the area's worst storm in fifty years. Blizzards covered the region with almost 24 inches (61 cm) of snow—yellow snow! It was yellow because strong winds swept up desert sand that mixed with the blowing snow.

For three days, sand and snow whipped through the air. It stung people's faces and piled up in drifts nearly 7 feet (2.1 m) deep. Temperatures dropped below −22°F (−30°C).

"This particular combination of a disaster is unheard of in living memory," commented Jim Robertson. He was a relief worker in China for the International Federation of Red

> ❝ *This particular combination of a* **disaster** *is unheard of in* **living memory**.❞
>
> *—Jim Robertson, a relief worker for the International Federation of Red Cross and Red Crescent Societies*

Cross and Red Crescent Societies. Robertson recalled a school bus that stopped to let a group of children off near their homes just before the blizzard started. *"Some of them never made it home,"* he said. *"There was no visibility, and the storm seems to have struck out of the blue."*

Up to 2.2 million people suffered in the disaster. The blizzard destroyed or damaged almost seventeen thousand mud and wood houses. Snowdrifts stranded people in villages. Residents didn't have enough food to eat or fuel to heat their homes.

Most people in Inner Mongolia depend on cows, goats, and other livestock for food. They also trade the animals for food, clothing, and other goods. More than 220,000 cattle died in the blizzard. Some froze to death. Others starved because farmers ran out of animal feed or could not get through the snow to feed the cattle.

Relief workers feared that 15 million more animals would starve to death if help didn't arrive quickly. They tried to bring in food for the animals and food, fuel, and blankets for the people. But they could not get through the snow. *"We couldn't reach the poorest [people],"* said Betty Lau, who helped the Red Cross deliver aid.

At least thirty-nine people froze to death. Making matters worse, at least fifteen more fierce snowstorms hit this area of China in the next two months.

These residents of Inner Mongolia lost much of their livestock during the snowstorms of January 2001.

35

People Helping People

BLIZZARDS LEAVE A TERRIBLE MESS THAT MUST BE CLEANED UP QUICKLY. OFTEN THE MESS IS SPREAD OVER A HUGE AREA. ONE SNOWSTORM IN 2006 AFFECTED MILLIONS OF PEOPLE FROM VIRGINIA TO MAINE. THE STORM HALTED TRANSPORTATION, CUT OFF ELECTRICITY, AND PREVENTED PEOPLE AT HOME FROM GETTING FRESH FOOD.

In a disaster, victims need help fast. Once people have been rescued, a disaster area often needs relief. Relief means providing shelter, transportation, food, water, or other help to reduce the amount of suffering. Residents may also need help with recovery—returning to normal life.

ROAD RESCUES

Blizzards often trap people in vehicles. Deep snow may drift over cars if drivers stop to wait for the weather to clear. Other cars may skid off the road and get stuck.

Without help, these travelers may freeze to death. However, ordinary police cars and fire trucks also can get stuck in deep snow. The U.S. Army may send Humvees to rescue motorists, as it did during a 2003 blizzard in Colorado. When the weather clears after a storm, helicopters may find and rescue drivers.

BURIED TURKEY

The Armistice Day Blizzard of 1940 left some families with no Thanksgiving turkey. Farmers in the Midwest had been raising turkeys to sell. But the blizzard on November 11 killed more than one million of those turkeys.

Red Cross workers dig out a buried car, looking for survivors after the blizzard of 1977 in Buffalo, New York.

"You can't even see. The highway is snowpacked, and it's slick and everybody's sliding off."

—Bill Kanitig, a sheriff in Kansas, reporting on a 2005 blizzard with drifts 6 feet (1.8 m) high

PLOW, PLOW, PLOW

Blizzard relief begins with snowplows and salt or sand trucks. Snowplows scrape snow from roads. Trucks spread salt and sand to keep roads from getting too slippery.

Snow removal work often begins even before the blizzard. When forecasters predict a blizzard, officials put plows and salt trucks on alert. They may drive out to busy roads and wait. As soon as the snow begins, they can get to work removing it.

Getting a head start is important. Blizzards can quickly pile up drifts 20 to 30 feet (6.1 to 9.1 m) high. If plows wait too long, the drifts may get so deep that even the snowplows get stuck.

BIG SNOW JOBS

Clearing snow from streets in a blizzard can be a huge job. In many cities, hundreds of miles of roads must be cleared. New York City has 6,300 miles (10,137 km) of streets. That's enough road to stretch to California and back. Cities in snowy areas call on hundreds of plows and salt trucks to cover all those roads. After a February 2006 blizzard in New York City, about 2,200 plows and 350 salt trucks hit the streets. Sometimes huge snowblowers also help clear highways by blowing snow off the road.

People want the snow plowed immediately so they can get back to work and schools can reopen. People can go shopping and buy food. But they often must wait. "This task will be enormous," Chicago mayor Richard Daley told residents after a big 1999 blizzard. "This is a major storm and the cleanup will take time, perhaps days."

RED CROSS RELIEF

During a blizzard, motels fill up fast with travelers. Thousands of others may need a place to stay until the weather clears. The American Red Cross, the largest U.S. relief organization, usually opens shelters for these travelers. Red Cross workers set up beds for people in schools or other buildings. The workers give food, soap, and toothbrushes to stranded travelers.

The Red Cross set up this relief shelter in
Oklahoma after a storm hit the area in
January 2007. People slept on cots at the
shelter until they could return home.

People stuck in airports and train stations also need relief. During the 2003 Colorado blizzard, about four thousand people were stranded at Denver International Airport. No help could reach the airport for two full days. Red Cross workers finally got through with hot meals for the hungry travelers.

In the worst blizzards, people may need help from the U.S. government. The government sent soldiers to help rescue stranded people during a severe blizzard in the Midwest in 1978. Army trucks with snowplows helped clear snow from roads. Military helicopters airlifted patients to hospitals. Some cities were snowbound for so long that stores ran out of food. Army helicopters and trucks brought in emergency food supplies.

PEOPLE POWER

Big machines aid in recovery work after a storm. City workers finish plowing the roads, including smaller streets that weren't plowed during the storm. Some snowy towns even have plows for the sidewalks. But residents must lend a hand. It takes muscle power to shovel snow from driveways and sidewalks. Some people in snowy areas own snowblowers to make clearing snow easier. A person pushes the snowblower, like a lawnmower, while it picks up snow and blows it off to the side through a chute.

In some places, laws require people to clear their sidewalks after a storm. The city can fine people fifty to one hundred dollars for not shoveling. Everyone must cooperate. If one family leaves snow on its sidewalks, everyone has a hard time getting through.

BEYOND SHOVELING

Cities began using plows to clear streets in the 1860s. Milwaukee, Wisconsin, was one of the first cities to plow its streets. Teams of horses pulled these first plows. Plows were also attached to the front of trains to clear a path on the railroad.

In the 1930s and 1940s, cities began spreading salt on roads to melt snow and ice. They also spread sand. Sand does not melt snow, but it makes it less slippery. Modern cities still use salt and sand. They also use saltlike materials that melt snow and ice better than salt does.

A U.S. Army Payloader removes snow in Buffalo, New York, in 2000. A lake-effect storm with blizzard conditions had dumped more than 2 feet (0.6 m) of snow on the area.

ELECTRIFYING WORK

Blizzards may knock down electric power poles and wires. Thousands of homes may be left cold and dark.

As soon as streets are clear, workers from the electric companies drive to areas without power. They reconnect broken wires and turn the lights back on. If there is great damage, electric companies from other areas may send their trucks to help.

Clear roads allow workers from cable and telephone companies to go fix their wires too. Then people will have TV, Internet, and phone service again.

RECOVERY PERIOD

The heavy snow in blizzards can damage the roofs on homes. When that happens, families may need a place to live for weeks or months, until repairs can be done. Sometimes the government provides money to help those families get by. Farmers also may need help recovering. Blizzards can kill whole herds of cattle. Thousands of chickens and other farm animals may die. Farmers may need money from the government to replace lost animals.

In the United States, however, most people recover from blizzards quickly. Life gets back to normal when the roads are clear and the lights go back on. Usually, by spring the blizzard is just a memory.

SNOWPLOW IN REVERSE

In the 1800s, cities hired workers to *keep* snow on the roads. People drove horse-drawn wagons over rough dirt roads in those days. In winter they switched to sleighs *(right)*—wagons with skis instead of wheels. Snow gave the roads a smooth surface for sleighing. Workers used special wagons to pack down the snow and fill in bare spots.

Electricity workers in Munster, Germany, repair a major electrical cable after it was damaged in a November 2005 blizzard. More than 250,000 people were without power following the blizzard.

A blizzard made driving slow and dangerous on this mountain pass between Andorra and France. People on a coach bus watched traffic crawl by after their bus became stuck.

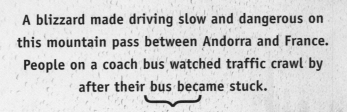

2005
EUROPE

Passengers on the bus were excited. They were heading for a ski vacation in Andorra, a tiny country between France and Spain. The passengers were happy when snow began to fall outside the bus. It meant good skiing conditions for their vacation. Soon the snow got heavier. The wind got stronger and whipped the snow into drifts.

At first the travelers were not too concerned. Caroline O'Sullivan was on the bus with her husband and two children. *"We passed cars that were stuck in the snow, but everything appeared OK,"* she recalled.

Then the bus got stuck on the road. It remained stuck all day and all night. Passengers had no food or water. They had to go to the bathroom outside in the snow while winds howled at 75 miles (121 km) per hour. *"We tried to keep our spirits up as best we could, but it was just awful,"* said O'Sullivan.

Blizzards in 2005 made travel conditions terrible all over Europe. During one storm in Britain, two hundred cars got stuck in snowdrifts 3 feet (0.9 m) deep. Police and fire squads helped clear roads and rescue travelers. *"As the cold and driving winds set in, some [stranded travelers] began to panic,"* reported Nick Grainger, a firefighter. *"They were wondering if they would ever get out [of the snow]."*

Rescue workers used plows to clear paths to the trapped cars. Then they used shovels to remove snow around the cars and free the trapped passengers. Grainger reported that they dug out each vehicle one at a time.

In southern Italy, where snow is rare, a blizzard trapped five hundred people in their cars for two days. Traveler Luigi Ruggiero remembered, *"We spent two nights in the cold, in the car, eating what we had with us—and drinking snow."*

The blizzards across Europe made life more difficult for people at home too. Snowdrifts blocked the roads into villages in Scotland, Spain, Poland, Slovakia, and other countries, isolating village residents. Wind knocked down electric power lines, and people were trapped in their houses without electricity for several days.

"It's a nightmare."

—a truck driver in Great Britain, where 12 inches (30 cm) of snow fell during one storm

This snowplow slid off the road during a particularly bad storm in Slovakia in 2005.

The Future

WHEN WE LEARN FROM DISASTERS, IT BECOMES EASIER TO COPE WITH FUTURE DISASTERS. THE LESSONS WE LEARN HELP US REDUCE THE DAMAGE FROM BLIZZARDS AND SPEED UP RECOVERY.

One of those lessons can be seen on the streets of New York and other big cities. Look up. Where are the telephone poles? What happened to the electric wires and the TV and Internet cables? The disastrous Great Blizzard of 1888 left New York's streets with broken wires tangled like spaghetti. The city decided to put those wires in a place safe from blizzards—buried in underground tunnels.

FOUR-WHEEL DRIVE VERSUS BLIZZARDS

Snow disasters have affected modern transportation. Many cities once had streetcar lines. These trains ran on rails in the street. They stopped every few blocks so people could get on and off. In the winter, heavy snow often blocked the rails. The Great Blizzard of 1888 even blocked New York's elevated streetcars. Blizzards were one reason why New York and other cities put their streetcars underground. The underground trains became modern subway and metro systems.

Past snowstorms also helped change the cars we drive. Sport-utility vehicles (SUVs) and four-wheel-drive vehicles are popular in part because they can drive through the snow better. In ordinary cars, the engine turns only one set of wheels—the front or the rear wheels. In most SUVs, the engine drives all four wheels, which gives the car better control in snow.

This Buffalo, New York, street is
filled with abandoned vehicles
following a November 2000 blizzard.

HOLD THE SALT

People use plows and salt to clear most roads. Salt is inexpensive and works well in keeping cars from skidding. However, road salt and other materials that melt ice can cause environmental damage. They get into the soil and may damage plants. They can make drinking water salty and unhealthy. Road salt also can hurt fish and other animals in rivers and lakes.

Scientists are trying to find replacements for road salt. The new material must be inexpensive, because millions of tons of it will be used every year. In addition, it must be safe for the environment.

SMART ROADS

New technology for building roads may reduce the need for plowing and salting in the future. Scientists are trying to develop "smart roads." These roads will be able to melt snow.

Experts already know how to make certain kinds of smart roads. Some streets have tiny pieces of a saltlike material mixed right into the asphalt. Cars driving over the road smash the pieces, releasing small amounts of the salty material. The material then helps to melt snow on the asphalt. However, this material is very expensive. So it is used only on small areas of a road, such as dangerous curves.

FORECASTING IN THE FUTURE

One of Earth's satellites may improve future blizzard predictions. This satellite measures ozone—a gas high in the air. It also shows air movement at the ozone level. These winds are higher than the conditions that other weather instruments can measure. The measurements give scientists more complete weather information. So they may be able to predict blizzards more accurately and further in advance.

Trucks such as this one spread salt or sand
onto the road to improve traction for
vehicles on icy and snowy roads.

SNOWPLOWS WITH A BRAIN

Snowplows may get smart in the future as well. Scientists are developing computer systems that help plows clear more snow. Less snow left on the road means less need for salt and sand.

A computer will work together with a new kind of plow blade. This blade will be made from movable pieces. The computer will sense how much snow is on the road. Then it will adjust the shape of the plow blade so that it can scoop up all the snow. Hundreds of adjustments will be made every minute.

The computer also will take the temperature of the road surface. That

information will determine how much salt must be spread on the road. A colder road will need more salt than a warmer one.

Residents of New York City *(left)* and Philadelphia *(below)* dig out of major snowstorms during the winter of 2005–2006.

DID YOU KNOW?

Many of the people who die in blizzards are adults who die from heart attacks while shoveling snow. Snow shoveling is hard work. Each shovelful of wet snow can weigh more than 20 pounds (9.1 kilograms). Only people in good physical condition who are used to exercise should shovel. Even then it is important to work slowly and take frequent breaks.

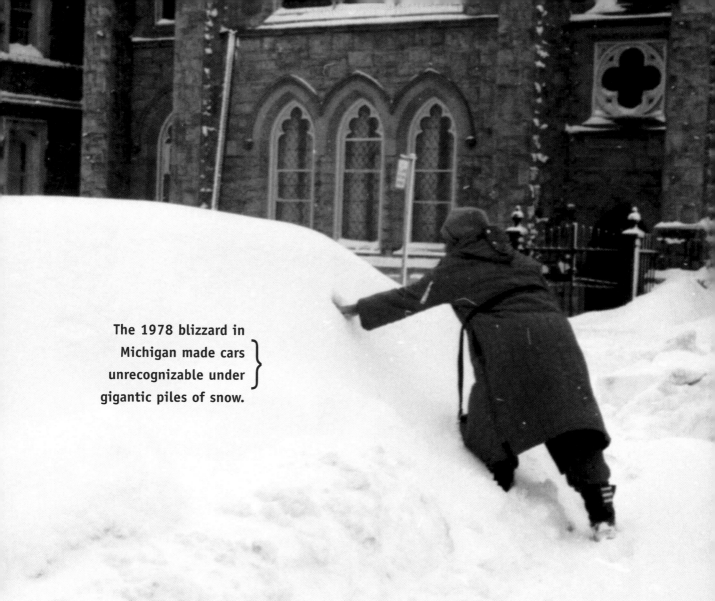

The 1978 blizzard in Michigan made cars unrecognizable under gigantic piles of snow.

"**That environment out there is as hostile as outer space.**"

—Ormond Danford, describing the weather outside his Michigan home during a 1978 blizzard

SNOWPLOWS WITH EYES

Plows must drive slowly in a blizzard. The blowing snow makes it difficult for snowplow drivers to see the road. They don't know what might be ahead of them. Cars could be stuck in the snow. People might be on the road waving for help.

In the future, snowplows may have radar systems, which use radio waves to detect objects. Images on a radar screen inside the truck would show plow drivers what's ahead of them. These plows could safely drive faster. Roads would be cleared more quickly during and after blizzards.

A FINE LINE IN FORECASTING

Computers may solve one of the hardest problems in forecasting blizzards. The problem involves deciding where to draw a line on weather maps. On one side of the line is heavy snow. On the other is heavy rain.

In a 2000 storm, forecasts for Raleigh, North Carolina, called for rain. But the rain-snow line prediction was slightly off. Raleigh got more than 20 inches (51 cm) of snow—its biggest snowfall on record.

That mistake happened because computers predicted conditions for fairly large areas. The areas were squares about 7.5 miles (12 km) wide. Scientists are working to predict blizzards and other storms for areas 1 or 2 miles (about 2 to 3 km) square. In the future, each neighborhood may know how severely a blizzard will hit its community.

AVOIDING THE BLIZZARD BLUES

Don't let the risk of a blizzard spoil your enjoyment of winter. Disastrous blizzards are rare. With modern weather forecasts, people usually have plenty of warning before a blizzard. And knowing how to prepare for blizzards can reduce your chances of being hurt by them.

PREPARING FOR BLIZZARDS

Home usually is the safest place during a blizzard. Start preparing when the weather forecast warns that a blizzard may be on the way.

Make sure to have:

- Enough bread, powdered milk, and other food to last for several days

- Canned foods that do not need cooking, and a can opener

- Medicine, baby supplies, and personal items that family members may need

- Food for pets

- Candles and matches, flashlights, a portable radio, and extra batteries

- Fully charged cell phone batteries

- Extra blankets and warm clothing

- Snow shovels

- Games and books, in case television and computers go out

Timeline

1717 Four snowstorms in one week create the Great Snow of 1717 in New England, with snowdrifts nearly 25 feet (7.6 m) deep.

1772 Future U.S. presidents Thomas Jefferson and George Washington write about a huge January snowstorm. The storm earned the name the Washington and Jefferson Snowstorm.

1846 Snowdrifts 40 feet (12 m) high trap the Donner party *(right)* for five months in a mountain pass in California's Sierra Nevadas.

1873 An April blizzard kills many farm animals in the Midwest.

1880–1881 Blizzards leave 11 feet (3.4 m) of snow on the South Dakota prairie where future author Laura Ingalls Wilder was growing up. In her book *The Long Winter*, Wilder tells how the community survived when the snow kept food supplies from arriving by train.

1888 On January 12, many schoolchildren are among the 235 people killed in a severe storm that became known as the Schoolchildren's Blizzard. On March 11–13, heavy snow and frigid winds in the Great Blizzard of 1888 kill more than 400 people on the East Coast of the United States.

1922 Heavy snow collapses the roof on the Knickerbocker Theater *(left)* in Washington, D.C., and kills nearly one hundred people in a blizzard called the Knickerbocker Storm.

1931 A school bus in southeastern Colorado becomes stuck in a blizzard for thirty-three hours. Five children and the bus driver freeze to death.

1940 A surprise November blizzard kills 150, including many hunters in Minnesota. They died from exposure—not having enough protection from the cold.

1949 Tens of thousands of cattle die in huge snowdrifts during storms in the Midwest.

1950 The Great Thanksgiving Storm hits twenty-two states and kills 383 people.

1956 Almost one thousand people in Europe die in horrible blizzards during January and February.

1972 A blizzard in Iran kills four thousand people.

1977 Strong winds and heavy snow produce drifts 30 feet (9.1 m) high in Buffalo, New York.

1978 The Blizzard of 1978 causes $1 billion in damage in New England. The New York City school district gets a snow day, an extremely rare occurrence.

1983 A blizzard in the eastern United States kills 270 people and causes up to $6 billion in damage.

1993 The Superstorm hits twenty-six states in March and causes $3 billion to $6 billion in damage.

1996 A January blizzard in the northeastern United States *(above)* kills 187 people.

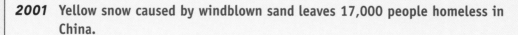

2001 Yellow snow caused by windblown sand leaves 17,000 people homeless in China.

2003 Thousands of travelers are stranded at airports when a mid-February blizzard dumps close to 2 feet (0.6 m) of snow on the eastern United States.

2005 A series of fierce blizzards all over Europe strands many travelers in cars and buses, requiring emergency vehicles and rescue workers to dig them out.

2006 Millions of people in New York City *(left)* and parts of New England are affected by a blizzard on February 11–12. For the first time in more than four years, officials close all three New York City area airports.

Glossary

Alberta Clippers: winter storms that move southeast from Canada and sometimes cause severe blizzards in the United States after they pick up moisture from the Great Lakes

blizzard: a severe winter storm in which winds of 35 miles (56 km) per hour or more blow snow through the air, reducing visibility to less than 0.25 mile (0.4 km) for at least three hours

frostbite: damage to the skin and body caused by exposure to cold temperatures

global warming: a gradual warming of Earth. Scientists think that air pollution chemicals are trapping heat around Earth, causing the warming.

hypothermia: abnormally low body temperature caused by exposure to cold weather. It can result in freezing to death if body temperature falls below 95°F (35°C).

jet streams: currents of air that flow high above Earth's surface and help to steer blizzards and other weather

lake-effect snowstorms: heavy snow that falls on land near a large lake as cold winds blow over the surface of the lake and pick up moisture

meteorologists: scientists who study the weather and make forecasts

nor'easter: a fierce storm that travels northeast and forms along the eastern coast of the United States. It often becomes a blizzard.

snowdrifts: piles of snow that build up when strong winds blow snow that is falling or already on the ground

visibility: the distance people can see, based on the weather and how clear the air is

whiteout: low visibility that occurs because of snow blowing through the air

windchill: an indication of how cold the air feels on skin, based on the air temperature and wind speed. Windchill is measured in degrees.

Places to Visit

During the winter months each year, a number of science museums and children's museums feature fun, interactive exhibits on snowstorms and winter storms. Check with the museums near you to find an exhibit you can visit.

The Buffalo Museum of Science, Buffalo, New York
http://www.sciencebuff.org
Check out the collection of Wilson "Snowflake" Bentley's photographs of individual snowflakes. Wilson Bentley pioneered the scientific technique of photographing snowflakes.

The Kansas City, Missouri, Public Library
http://www.kclibrary.org
This library has multiple articles about the January 1888 storm known as the Schoolchildren's Blizzard.

Laura Ingalls Wilder Memorial Society, De Smet, South Dakota
http://www.liwms.com
Visit two of Laura Ingalls Wilder's homes on the prairie featured in *The Long Winter*.

Washington Crossing State Park, in Titusville, New Jersey
http://www.state.nj.us/dep/parksandforests/parks/washcros.html
On December 25, 1776, amid a violent snowstorm, Revolutionary War general (and future president) George Washington and his Continental Army crossed the Delaware River here. They marched through the night to defeat opposing troops in the Battle of Trenton. Stop by the visitor center to see paintings that show the snows of 1777.

Source Notes

4 *Seattle Times*, "Blizzard Smothers East Coast: 'It's No Man's Land Out There,'" February 18, 2003.

4 Robert Ingrassia, "Blizzard of '03 Storms into City," *New York Daily News*, February 18, 2003.

5 *Seattle Times*, "Blizzard Smothers East Coast."

5 Tom Avril, "Colliding Systems Fueled Beastly 'Blizzard of '03,'" *State College (PA) Centre Daily Times*, February 18, 2003.

5 *Seattle Times*, "Blizzard Smothers East Coast."

9 Cotton Mather, *Diary of Cotton Mather, 1681–1724* (Boston: Society of Boston, 1911).

10 Meta Lilienthal, "Blizzard of 1888—Memoir of Meta Lilienthal," *Virtual New York*, 2001, http://www.vny.cuny.edu/Search/search_res_text.php?id=426 (June 26, 2007).

10 A. C. Chadbourne, "Blizzard of 1888—'Blizzard Men' Testimony," *Virtual New York*, 2001, http://www.vny.cuny.edu/Search/search_res_text.php?id=394 (June 26, 2007).

11 Shamgar Babcock, "Blizzard of 1888—'Blizzard Men' Testimony," *Virtual New York*, 2001, http://www.vny.cuny.edu/Search/search_res_text.php?id=389 (June 26, 2007).

11 Meta Lilienthal, "Blizzard of 1888—Memoir of Meta Lilienthal."

17 Herbert Smith, "Blizzard of 1888—'Blizzard Men' Testimony," *Virtual New York*, 2001, http://www.vny.cuny.edu/Search/search_res_text.php?id=400 (June 26, 2007).

18 Dennis Anderson, "1940 Armistice Day Blizzard," *Minneapolis Star Tribune*, November 8, 2000.

18 Mark Steil, "The Winds of Hell," *Minnesota Public Radio*, November 10, 2000, http://news.minnesota. publicradio.org/features/2005/11/10_steilm_ windsofhell/ (May 18, 2007).

19 Ibid.

19 Ibid.

19 Jane Otto, "Armistice Day Blizzard: A Storm Like No Other," *Winstead Herald Journal*, November 8, 2004, http://www.herald-journal.com/archives/2004/stories/snow.html (May 18, 2007).

19 Mark Steil, "The Winds of Hell."

24 Lindsay Riddell, "Family Recalls Blizzard Birthday: Helicopter Transported Snowed-in Mom to Hospital," *Chattanooga Times Free Press*, March 9, 2003.

25 Jack Harmon and Jack Warner, "Blizzard of 1993: Roads Clearing in N. Georgia Military Vehicles Help Reach Hard-hit Locations," *Atlanta Journal-Constitution*, March 18, 1993.

25 Curt Simmons and Elisa Willis, "Aftermath: 'The Damage Is Awesome,'" *Newsday*, March 16, 1993.

25 Monte R. Young, "For Some, Snow Day Brings Payday," *Newsday*, March 15, 1993.

25 Riddell, "Family Recalls Blizzard Birthday."

33 Ron Riechmann, "Blizzard of '78: Worst-Ever New England Snow Storm Leaves Vivid Memories and Lessons," *United Press International*, February 3, 1983.

34 Solveig Olafsdottir, "Freak Blizzard Hits Nomadic Herdsmen in Inner Mongolia," *International Federation of Red Cross and Red Crescent Societies*, January 25, 2001, http://www.ifrc.org/docs/news/01/012501/ (September 28, 2006).

34 Ibid.

35 *Kyodo News Service* (Japan), "Worst Blizzards in 50 Years Devastate Xinjiang," February 23, 2001.

35 Olafsdottir, "Freak Blizzard Hits Nomadic Herdsmen in Inner Mongolia."

37 CBS/AP, "Highways Closed, Travelers Stuck," *CBS News*, November 28, 2005, http://www.cbsnews.com/stories/2005/11/28/national/main1077377_page2.shtml (September 28, 2006).

38 Anthony Colarossi and Anthony Burke Boylan, "Winter Piles It On: Snowfall Snarls Streets, Slams Brakes on Air Travel: Worst Storm in 20 Years Means Days of Digging Out," *Chicago Tribune*, January 3, 1999.

44 Ann Mooney, "Frozen for 24 Hours; 45 Irish Tourists Trapped in Storm on Coach," *Mirror* (London), February 15, 2005.

44 Ibid.

45 Tom Kelly, "200 Cars Marooned; Pensioners' Six-Hour Ordeal in the Snow," *Daily Mail* (London), December 31, 2005.

45 BBC, "Heavy Snow Brings Chaos to Europe," *BBC News*, January 28, 2005, http://news.bbc.co.uk/2/hi/europe/4216751.stm (November 1, 2006).

45 CBC, "U.K. Struggles Through Winter Weather," *CBC News*, December 30, 2005, http://www.cbc.ca/world/story/2005/12/30/ukweather051230.html (June 8, 2007).

51 Kathy Gibbons and Marta Hepler Drahos, "The Great Blizzard of 1978," *Traverse City (MI) Record Eagle*, January 27, 1998, http://www.record-eagle.com/feech/blizz78/27bliz.htm (May 18, 2007).

Selected Bibliography

Allaby, Michael. *Blizzards*. New York: Facts on File, 1997.

Allen, Oliver E. *New York, New York*. New York: Atheneum, 1990.

Brandt, Nat. "The Great Blizzard of '88." *American Heritage*, February 1977, 33–41.

Burt, Christopher C. *Extreme Weather: A Guide & Record Book*. New York: W. W. Norton & Co., 2004.

Cosgrove, Brian. *Eyewitness: Weather*. New York: Dorling Kindersley, 2004.

Davis, Lee. *Natural Disasters*. New York: Facts on File, 2002.

Denver Rocky Mountain News. "The Survivors." *Colorado Millennium 2000*. 1999. http://www
.denver-rmn.com/millennium/survivor.shtml
(February 17, 2006).

Edwards, Diane. "Greetings from Antarctica!" *Project Dragonfly*. December 13, 2003. http://www.units
.muohio.edu/dragonfly/snow/mcmurdo.shtml
(February 13, 2006).

Engelbert, Phillis. *Dangerous Planet: The Science of Natural Disasters, Vol. 1*. Detroit: U.X.L., 2001.

FEMA. "Are You Ready?" *Federal Emergency Management Association*. March 21, 2006.
http://www.fema.gov/areyouready/winter.shtm
(March 27, 2006).

Laskin, David. *The Children's Blizzard*. New York: HarperCollins, 2004.

Massachusetts Foundation for the Humanities. "Blizzard Paralyzes Massachusetts." *Mass Moments*. February 9, 2007. http://www.massmoments.org/
moment.cfm?mid=45 (July 17, 2007).

Murphy, Jim. *Blizzard!* New York: Scholastic, 2000.

National Geographic Society. *Restless Earth: Disasters of Nature*. Washington, DC: National Geographic Society, 1997.

New York Times. "Missing Put at 6,000 in Iranian Blizzard." February 11, 1972, 4.

NSIDC. "Notable Winter Snowstorms: Historical List." *National Snow and Ice Data Center*. 2006.
http://nsidc.org/snow/blizzard/storms.html
(March 1, 2006).

Smith, Donald. "La Niña Returns, Bringing Blizzards and Misery." *National Geographic News*, December 9, 2000. http://news.nationalgeographic.com/
news/2000/12/1209_blizzard.html (February 17, 2006).

Spignesi, Stephen J. *The 100 Greatest Disasters of All Time*. New York: Kensington Publishing Corp., 2002.

Stevens, William K. *The Change in the Weather: People, Weather, and the Science of Climate*. New York: Delacorte Press, 1999.

Weather Channel. "Storm Encyclopedia: Blizzards." *The Weather Channel*. 2006.
http://www.weather.com/encyclopedia/
winter/blizzard.html (February 13, 2006).

Further Resources

BOOKS

Nonfiction

Barnard, Bryn. *Dangerous Planet: Natural Disasters That Changed History*. New York: Crown Publishers, 2003. Barnard discusses significant historical disasters and explains how global warming may cause more natural disasters.

Martin, Jacqueline Briggs. *Snowflake Bentley*. Boston: Houghton Mifflin, 1998. Read the true story of Wilson Bentley, who developed techniques of photography to show the world his discoveries of the shapes of snowflakes.

Newson, Lesley. *Devastation: The World's Worst Natural Disasters*. New York: DK Publishing, 1998. This book contains vivid images of many of Earth's natural disasters and the changes those disasters cause.

Sandler, Martin. *America's Great Disasters*. New York: HarperCollins, 2003. Sandler writes about a number of disasters, including the Great Blizzard of 1888 and how citizens recovered from it.

Vogel, Carole Garbury. *Nature's Fury: Eyewitness Reports of Natural Disaster*. New York: Scholastic, 2000. This book examines the horror of thirteen natural disasters.

Wilder, Laura Ingalls. *The Long Winter*. New York: Harper Collins, 1940. Join Laura as she tells the remarkable true story of her family's survival during the harsh winter of 1880–1881, which left many people close to starving on the prairie.

Fiction

Hart, Alison. *Anna's Blizzard*. Atlanta: Peachtree Publishers, 2005. When the schoolhouse roof collapses during the January 1888 blizzard, Anna and her pony lead the teacher and students to safety.

Kehret, Peg. *Blizzard Disaster*. New York: Pocket Books. 1998. Warren Spalding and Betsy Tyler time-travel back to November 11, 1940, to learn about the Armistice Day Blizzard in Minnesota.

Korman, Gordon. *Everest: Book One: The Contest*. New York: Scholastic. 2002. Four young boys attempt to be the youngest people to climb Mount Everest. Join them as they struggle through incredibly harsh weather. *Book Two: The Climb* and *Book Three: The Summit* follow in this series.

Myers, Edward. *Climb or Die*. New York: Hyperion Books for Children, 1994. After the Darcy's car crashes in a blizzard in Colorado, the parents are badly hurt. The children must climb up the mountain to a weather station to get help.

WEBSITES AND FILMS

Battling a Blizzard

http://www.kidzworld.com/site/p149.htm
This site provides science info, history, and other fun facts about blizzards, and it includes links to other weather sites for students.

Blizzards and Winter Weather

http://eo.ucar.edu/webweather/blizzardhome.html
This website is packed with interesting information about how blizzards form and how they affect people's lives.

The Digital Snow Museum

http://wintercenter.homestead.com/photoindex
.html
Look at images from many past blizzards, dating back to 1717.

FEMA for Kids: Winter Storms

http://www.fema.gov/kids/wntstrm.htm
Learn all about winter storms from the Federal Emergency Management Agency.

Ice and Snow

http://www.units.muohio.edu/dragonfly/snow
Find out about winter in Antarctica.

Interactive Weather Maker

http://www.scholastic.com/kids/weather/
Create (and end!) your own blizzard by using this interactive weather site.

Severe Weather and Natural Disasters: Winter Storms

http://teacher.scholastic.com/activities/wwatch/
winter_storms/index.htm
This interactive site provides plenty of information presented in a student-friendly way.

SnowSchool: Where Is SnowSchool?

http://www.snowschool.org/where
Find a SnowSchool program in your area. The programs help children learn about ecology and the environment through winter activities.

Weather Wiz Kids: Winter Storms

http://www.weatherwizkids.com/winter_storms
.htm
Meteorologist Crystal Wicker answers many questions about winter storms. Learn about winter weather in your area, and make your own barometer.

Blizzards: Whiteout! New York: A&E Entertainment. 2001. Find out about the devastating 1888 blizzards in the United States. Also learn about two famous Chicago blizzards, in 1967 and 1979.

March of the Penguins. Washington, DC: National Geographic, 2005. Watch the incredible survival techniques that emperor penguins use to endure blizzards in the harsh climate of Antarctica.

Nor'easters: Killer Storms. New York: A&E Entertainment. 2006. Find out all about the violent winter storms that strike New England. First-person accounts and dramatic footage make this an exciting show.

Wrath of God: Buffalo Blizzard: Siege and Survival. New York: History Channel, 2001. This storm lasted six days in January 1977 and caused President Carter to declare nine counties in upstate New York as federal disaster areas.

Index

Photo Acknowledgments

The images in this book are used with the permission of: AP Photo/Mary Altaffer, p. 1; © Jodi Hilton/Getty Images, p. 3; © Reuters/CORBIS, pp. 4, 14, 34, 41, 47; © David Hume Kennerly/Getty Images, pp. 5, 13 (background); © Raymond Gehman/CORBIS, p. 7; © Sandy Ciric/Getty Images, p. 9; Library of Congress, pp. 10 (LC-USZ62-43668), 42 (LC-USZ62-113462); AP Photo/Arthur H. Fisher, p. 11; © SIU/Visuals Unlimited, p. 12; © Bill Hauser/Independent Picture Service, p. 13; © CORBIS, pp. 15, 17; Minnesota Historical Society, p. 18; Photo by *Minneapolis Star Journal*, Minnesota Historical Society, p. 19; © Syracuse Newspapers/The Image Works, p. 21 (top); © China Photos/Getty Images, p. 21 (bottom); AP Photo/Justine Sutcliffe, p. 24; © HAWKINS KEN/CORBIS SYGMA, p. 25; Courtesy of the National Oceanic and Atmospheric Administration Central Library Photo Collection, pp. 26, 31; © Scientifica/Visuals Unlimited, p. 27; © Chris Cheadle/Photographer's Choice/Getty Images, p. 28; © Aaron Mccoy/Robert Harding World Imagery/Getty Images, p. 29; © GK Hart/Vikki Hart/The Image Bank/Getty Images, p. 30; © David Jay Zimmerman/CORBIS, pp. 31 (background), 55 (bottom); AP Photo, p. 33; AP Photo/Wang Yebiao, Xinhua, p. 35; Courtesy of the American Red Cross. All rights reserved in all countries, p. 37; © Brandi Simons/Getty Images, p. 39; © Ralph Orlowski/Getty Images, p. 43; © Ashley Cooper/Alamy, p. 44; © Martin Baumann/AFP/Getty Images, p. 45; © Kul Bhatia/zefa/CORBIS, p. 49; © Spencer Platt/Getty Images, p. 50 (top); © William Thomas Cain/Getty Images, p. 50 (bottom); Walter P. Reuther Library, Wayne State University, p. 51; AP Photo/Bizuayehu Tesfaye, p. 53 (background); © Bettmann/CORBIS, p. 54 (both); AP Photo/Kathy Willens, p. 55 (top).

Front Cover: © Colin McPherson/CORBIS (main), © Astromujoff/Riser/Getty Images (snow effect); Back Cover: Minnesota Historical Society.

About the Authors

Michael Woods is a science and medical journalist in Washington, D.C., who has won many national writing awards. Mary B. Woods is a school librarian. Their past books include the eight-volume Ancient Technology series. The Woodses have four children. When not writing, reading, or enjoying their grandchildren, the Woodses travel to gather material for future books.